50 STEAM LABS

- **S** Science
- **T** Technology
- **E** Engineering
- **A** Art
- **M** Mathematics

50 STEAM Labs

ABOUT

INTENT & PURPOSE: The projects within are frameworks for STEAM activities for Elementary and Middle School level students. Depending on the ability levels of the students involved, younger or older students might also be able to do these projects with added guidance for younger students or altered expectations for older students.

PROJECTS: Each of the 50 STEAM Labs will include ideas for Science, Technology, Engineering, Art, and Mathematics components for the thematic project. It is not expected that every student will complete all 5 components for each project. Rather, picking and choosing 3-4 of the 5 components. Although, students may very well want to do all 5 parts of the project.

GRADING & STANDARDS: There are no grading rubrics attached to these projects. Nor have standards been included. Because these projects are intended for a wide grade range, it was impossible to denote specific standards for each project. It is best to determine on your own what sort of grades you wish to assign to each project or each component within projects.

COPYRIGHT: All art and designs inside are created by Andrew Frinkle, with the exception of the gear design, which is courtesy of vectoropenstock.com The projects contained within are (C) 2017 MediaStream Press and Andrew Frinkle. They may not be duplicated, sold, hosted online, or repackaged for sale or distributed for free.

PERSONAL USE: A limited license is granted to the purchaser of this volume, either digital or physical copy, to copy and use this book at home or in school for educational purposes only. It is a single-teacher license and should not be shared between classes.

50 STEAM Labs

Fairy Homes   01

 **SCIENCE:** Learn about habitats. Determine what resources you think a fairy would require in his or her habitat. Make sure to determine what plants or animals/insects the fairy might want to live around. Collect the resources.

 **TECHNOLOGY:** Research your habitat and design ideas. Type up a short story about fairies or your fairy. Incorporate lighting if possible.

 **ENGINEERING:** Design and build the habitat using available resources. Create a 3-dimensional diorama or enclosure from scratch, or use a terrarium, small pet cage, or fishbowl.

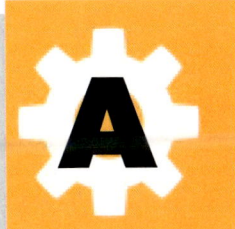 **ART:** Create and decorate the habitat. Optionally. create a fairy language and leave miniature notes or glyphs around the habitat.

 **MATHEMATICS:** Determine the measurements of your habitat. Calculate volume. Volume of air, plant mass, water, soil, or other materials could also be calculated. Create a graphic or chart displaying the measurement data.

(c) 2017 MediaStream Press

50 STEAM Labs

The Collectors — 02

SCIENCE: Gather a collection and classify it. It can be a collection of anything, such as stickers, coins, rocks, bugs, leaves, or even toy characters. Create a series of dichotomous questions, criteria, or classification rules to follow. Rules should be consistent. and complete enough to handle most or all situations.

TECHNOLOGY: Type up or create a flowchart, slideshow, or poster to showcase the rules and criteria you use to classify your objects.

ENGINEERING: Build a box or container for your collection. You might need tools, glue, and a variety of materials to complete your collection.

ART: Design and decorate your collection box, poster, or container.

MATHEMATICS: After completing your collection, you can graph and chart the amount of objects in each category or group of your collection.

(c) 2017 MediaStream Press

50 STEAM Labs

Sports Fans   03

SCIENCE: Research forces and motion. Determine which physical forces are at play in this sport or activity and how. Kinetic and potential energy, as well as friction, drag, wind resistance, and other forces may be a good place to start.

TECHNOLOGY: Create a map of locations where your sport is played, where sports teams are located, or where championship teams have come from.

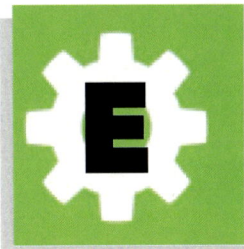

ENGINEERING: Create a model version of one or more of the materials or gear involved in the sport. Try to make them as accurate as possible, using similar materials when possible.

ART: Design helmets, jerseys, or other athletic equipment for the sport you chose.

MATHEMATICS: Create a list of math facts about your sport, such as: How many pro or semi-pro teams are there? How large is the field? How much does the ball weigh? How long are the skis?

(c) 2017 MediaStream Press

50 STEAM Labs

Hero Worship — 04

SCIENCE: Research the science behind your hero's powers, such as night vision (types of animal eyes), super strength (muscles), flight (4 forces of flight), or control of earth (tectonics).

TECHNOLOGY: Scan in your illustrations and make digital copies of them. You can also publish and modify your pictures to create an entire poster or comic.

ENGINEERING: Make a diorama or model of your character using his or her powers. For example, you could create a diorama with a suspended miniature version of your character flying over hilltops through clouds and the sky.

ART: Illustrate a comic panel, an entire book, a poster, or at least a detailed image of your character in his or her costume. You can also create a back story and secret identities.

MATHEMATICS: Determine key math facts affecting your hero, such as his or her vital stats and the measurable limitations of their powers. How fast can he or she fly? How tall is he or she? How much weight can he or she lift?

(c) 2017 MediaStream Press

50 STEAM Labs

Lunar Calendars 05

SCIENCE: Research the moon phases and how they are involved in different calendars in the world.

TECHNOLOGY: Create a custom calendar. Use our regular 12-month calendar, or create a new one based on the lunar or solar patterns. Additionally, new names for days or months could be created.

ENGINEERING: Print, create, and/or assemble your completed calendar. Binding it with a spiral, glue, or plastic binding comb is a plus.

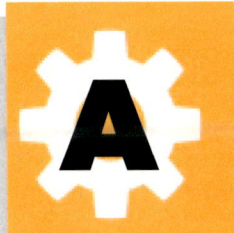
ART: Decorate a calendar. Seasonal or monthly themes are a plus.

MATHEMATICS: Research and collect statistics about the number of days, weeks, months, hours, minutes, etc... in a year. Find other divisions of time, such as nanoseconds, decades, centuries, and more. Also, statistics about the moon could be collected.

(c) 2017 MediaStream Press

50 STEAM Labs

Hidden in the Grass — 06

SCIENCE: Research and catalog the species of plants and animals found in a 1 square meter or 1 square yard of land at a school, park, beach, forest, or at your home. Also, catalog nonliving things, such as dirt, types of rocks, etc... Classify them in a sensible manner.

TECHNOLOGY: Create charts and tables of the different species and objects found in your section of land.

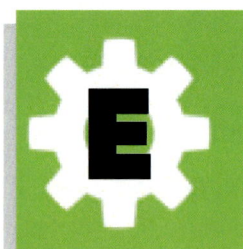

ENGINEERING: Measure and rope off the best section of property available in the given location. Carefully put down stakes and ropes to denote the edges of the piece.

ART: When possible, collect natural samples of the findings. Otherwise, illustrate them. Samples can be arranged logically on a decorated poster or in another sensible storage method.

MATHEMATICS: Use math to predict and calculate the number of objects in your section. It would not be necessary to count every blade of grass in the section; rather, count how many pieces are in a fraction of your section and multiply to determine an estimate for the total section. Charts and tables should be created to hold your data.

(c) 2017 MediaStream Press

50 STEAM Labs

Architects   07

SCIENCE: Research home designs and blueprints, as well as the building process of homes in your area. Are they built from lumber primarily, brick, or concrete block? What sort of storm windows, earthquake, or wind concerns are there to take into effect?

TECHNOLOGY: Take your drawn blueprint or design, scan it in or take a picture of it. Add words and details to it with software. Print it out or share it with your class or peers online.

ENGINEERING: Design a blueprint of your house or of a dream house you might build some day. Try to add all the rooms you will need, doors, windows, closets, stairs, porches, and all of the major requirements of a home.

ART: Decorate and build a 3D model of your house. Try to build landscaping in the yard as well.

MATHEMATICS: Multiply out stats like square footage, lengths of interior and exterior walls, and the area in each room. Using scale units on graph paper can help with this, such as 1 square = 4 sq ft. The amount of flooring, paint, and other materials can also be calculated.

(c) 2017 MediaStream Press

50 STEAM Labs

Little Critters — 08

SCIENCE: Research any animal. Find out as much as possible about it, and use that information to create a scale model of it.

TECHNOLOGY: Use technology and computers to research, as well as the school or local library. To accompany the model, create a slideshow, typed report, or other multimedia presentation.

ENGINEERING: Design and build the scale model of the animal with available materials, either purchased, provided, or scavenged from home and school.

ART: Decorate the model to make it as lifelike as possible, keeping an eye out for skin coverings, coloration, general shape of the animal, and other major features and characteristics.

MATHEMATICS: Design the model to scale. Depending on the size of the organism, you might actually do a blown-up scale version of it, or you might have to do a much smaller version of it, if the animal is particularly large. Keep scale consistent through the model. Also, numerical facts about the animal can be collected and presented.

(c) 2017 MediaStream Press

50 STEAM Labs

Custom Textbooks 09

SCIENCE: Research a science topic of your choice. Take notes and prepare a story, article, or self-published informative piece about it.

TECHNOLOGY: Type, arrange, edit, and add illustrations and visuals to your research piece. Work collaboratively if possible to fill an entire volume with pieces of work on a similar topic.

ENGINEERING: Bind your self-published piece. Use plastic comb binding machines, make a spiral-bound notebook, or use a 3-ring binder and hole puncher.

ART: Decorate the interior and the cover of your textbook.

MATHEMATICS: Add graphs, data, and charts to your textbook.

(c) 2017 MediaStream Press

50 STEAM Labs

Fashion Designer   10

SCIENCE: Research how different fabrics are made, or, if the fabric is manmade, the chemicals and processes involved in its creation.

TECHNOLOGY: Try to create your design with art and design software. Sketches can also be scanned in and notes or instructions can be added digitally. Optionally, use a sewing machine, if possible. Supervision will likely me required.

ENGINEERING: Take apart an old or discarded garment to look at how patterns could be made from it. Look at how garments such as shirts, dresses, or jackets are assembled.

ART: Sketch and design a garment for a person or a doll.

MATHEMATICS: Design the garment, identifying the geometric shapes and pieces required. Use measurements to create it accurately, with little waste. Preplanning allows for the most efficient use of materials. Measure, plan, and then cut.

(c) 2017 MediaStream Press

50 STEAM Labs

Recycled Gardens 11

SCIENCE: Research vertical gardens, residential gardening, raised bed gardens, and other limited space gardening techniques. Also, check which species of plants compliment each other when grown together. Find a good combination to grow in your garden. Additionally, check the water, spacing, and lighting requirements for each plant you plan on using.

TECHNOLOGY: Research online and find picture to get ideas for gardening with recycled materials. Draw up plans for your own garden. Take pictures and share with peers after it is completed.

ENGINEERING: Using recycled materials as much as possible, build a container garden for a windowsill, a patio, porch, or other limited space area. Design for drainage, careful use of water, sunlight, and growth.

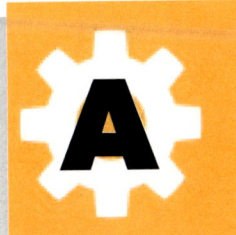

ART: Sketch and draw your garden prior to building. Decorate as you make it and after you finish it.

MATHEMATICS: Calculate the amount of materials needed, especially gravel, perlite, potting soil, water, tubing, etc... After the garden is started, germination rates can be calculated for each seed type.

(c) 2017 MediaStream Press

50 STEAM Labs

Recycled Homes   12

SCIENCE: Research types of birds in your area. Determine what sort of home they might require. Also determine their diets and other requirements, so you can provide the best possible home for them.

TECHNOLOGY: Research online and find picture to get ideas for building birdhouses from recycled materials. Draw up plans for your own birdhouse. Take pictures and share with peers after it is completed.

ENGINEERING: Using recycled materials as much as possible, build a birdhouse. Make sure it has proper airflow, size, and a way to mount or hang it.

ART: Sketch and draw your birdhouse prior to building. Decorate as you make it and after you finish it. It can even be camouflaged in to better fit the environment.

MATHEMATICS: Calculate the amount of materials needed to make the birdhouse. Take careful measurements. Hang it from a proper height to avoid predators and pests.

(c) 2017 MediaStream Press

50 STEAM Labs

Crash Testers 13

SCIENCE: Research the forces involved in car crashes. Things like momentum, inertia, and velocity are great words to start with.

TECHNOLOGY: Use the internet to research car crash testing and crash test ratings, as well as types of crashes. Determine what sorts of safety measures have been built into many cars.

ENGINEERING: Design and build a scale model of a car or a series of models from household and office materials. Place a small character or doll inside it. Device a series of crush from different angles and/or crash tests at different speeds.

ART: Sketch and design your car or vehicle. Try multiple designs and styles. Decorate the finished model.

MATHEMATICS: Measure the pressures (or amount of weight) it can take from different angles before the characters are squished by the beams and frame of the car. Chart and record data.

(c) 2017 MediaStream Press

50 STEAM Labs

Cold Feelings   14

SCIENCE: Research thermal energy and heat transfer. Also look into thermal conductors and insulators. Determine which materials best transfer hot and cold. Use available samples of several materials to create an insulator.

TECHNOLOGY: Use thermometers to record data. Digital thermometers or temperature probes that dump data straight to a PC or laptop are even better. Create graphs and data charts on a spreadsheet or other piece of software.

ENGINEERING: Design two or more identically-sized insulated boxes out of different materials. They will be used to hold either a cup of hot water, or a cup of ice. Measure temperature changes over 5, 10, 15, 30, or 60 minute intervals.

ART: Sketch out and design the projects before making them. Decorate them if you want.

MATHEMATICS: After creating your insulated boxes, measure and record temperature changes. Create charts. Plot and graph data to determine the rates of change and other statistics. Test more than once to create averages.

(c) 2017 MediaStream Press

50 STEAM Labs

Colony Ships

  15

SCIENCE: Research space shuttles, spacecraft, and theoretical designs for interplanetary vessels. Also research how humans survive in space and what it takes to get into space and safely land.

TECHNOLOGY: Use NASA and other space agency websites to learn more about space travel and colonization ideas. Independent space agencies can also be researched for ideas. Look at the historical missions versus upcoming and planned missions for the future.

ENGINEERING: Design a colony vessel to take humans from Earth to an asteroid, moon, or planet in our solar system. Make sure to include everything that humans would need to survive.

ART: Make up artistic space meal menus for the colonists. Also create artistic renderings of space vessels and early colonies.

MATHEMATICS: Research the distances between the planets in our solar system and when their orbits bring them closest. Use math to calculate the speeds required to travel between them and the travel times. Use this information to also calculate the supplies required for the trip and to sustain the crew until a new food/water supply can be established.

(c) 2017 MediaStream Press

50 STEAM Labs

Better Keyboards — 16

SCIENCE: Learn about tendons, muscles, ligaments, and nerves, and how they are all interrelated. Research repetitive stress injuries. How are keyboards, cell phones, and other technologies causing injuries?

TECHNOLOGY: Look up different keyboard arrangements and designs online, such as QWERTY, DVORAK, and COLEMAK. Also look at various keyboard designs.

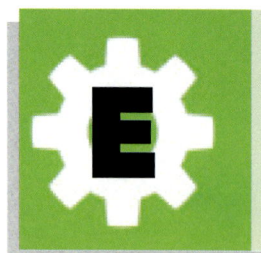

ENGINEERING: Design a model of a better keyboard. Think about how the keys should be arranged. What new keys should be added and which ones should be omitted?

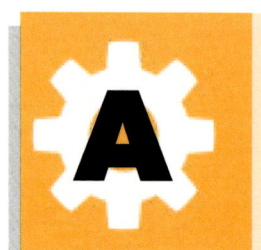

ART: Make your keyboard look good! Make it ergonomic and cool looking. No one wants a boring old white keyboard.

MATHEMATICS: Determine which keys are used most often. Look for the most common letters in simple passages. Use this to help determine how keys should be arranged. Also, chart and graph the most common characters in stories, poems, or other written pieces.

(c) 2017 MediaStream Press

50 STEAM Labs

Skilled Trades   17

SCIENCE: Research plumbing, heating/cooling, electrical, welding, or other skilled trades careers.

TECHNOLOGY: Look up how-to videos for a particular field. Take notes, learn, and practice in a safer, mock-up version of the trade.

ENGINEERING: Carefully (with supervision when appropriate), do a mock-up version of the work that skilled tradesmen might do. For example, use rubber tubing to plumb a project, run wires to batteries and light bulbs, use a hot glue gun to practice welding techniques, etc...

ART: Present your creation in a art fair style fashion. Make signs or boards explaining what you did and make it look good!

MATHEMATICS: Research the number of jobs and other job-related facts for a particular skilled trade, such as pipefitting, plumbing, HVAC, electrical, welding, etc... How many years of experience are required? What sort of training? What sort of pay and compensation are expected?

(c) 2017 MediaStream Press

50 STEAM Labs

Better Trash 18

SCIENCE: Research waste management, as well as recycling and natural resources that are renewable/nonrenewable.

TECHNOLOGY: Find information about your local recycling programs, solid waste, yard waste, and also recycling of things like batteries and CFL lightbulbs. Make a presentation about your family's recycling and waste habits.

ENGINEERING: Design a better package for something you or your family buys regularly. How can the package be more ergonomic, safer, less wasteful, or more environmentally friendly? Another option is to create a waste disposal unit or garbage can that is easier or better to use.

ART: Make an art object from recycled materials.

MATHEMATICS: Calculate the fractions or percentages of your household waste that fall into common categories like: recyclable plastics (what types and numbers?), cardboard and paper, food waste, yard waste, etc... Use this information to make a chart, graph, or presentation.

(c) 2017 MediaStream Press

50 STEAM Labs

 # Ergonomics  19

 **SCIENCE:** Research simple and compound machines. Also research a variety of designs of the tool you want to improve. For example, there are many kinds of shovels. If you were trying to improve one, does your idea already exist? Also, which types of simple machines are present in your tool?

 **TECHNOLOGY:** Create a slideshow or other presentation piece to use in your product pitch for your improved product.

 **ENGINEERING:** Make a common household, garage, or office tool more ergonomic. After designing a way to make it more comfortable to use, actually make a prototype.

 **ART:** Sketch and design the product first. Then make a product pitch, as if you were trying to sell your idea to a group of investors. You can even compete for imaginary funding against other peers to see who has the most promising designs.

 **MATHEMATICS:** Develop a cost plan as part of your pitch and product research. How much would it cost to implement your alterations? How much would it sell for? What sort of profit could be made if you sold 100, 1000, or even more?

(c) 2017 MediaStream Press

50 STEAM Labs

Like Clockwork — 20

SCIENCE: Research gears and mechanical devices. Pay special attention to camshafts in modern engines, steam locomotives, and even gears within clocks.

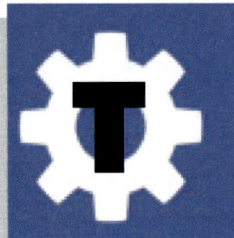

TECHNOLOGY: If possible, take apart a piece of machinery with gears in it, such as a wall clock. Obviously, take apart a safe machine, and do it with proper tools and supervision.

ENGINEERING: Create your own gear-driven device. Use wood, plastic, cardboard, or other available materials to create gears that push and drive other parts of the device to accomplish something.

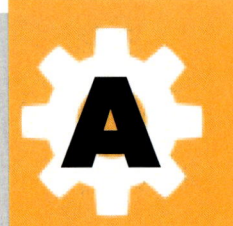

ART: Make your device look awesome. Make it look super modern, or paint it bronze or metallic colors, age it, and make it look antique.

MATHEMATICS: Calculate gear ratios. Same size gears turn at a 1:1 ratio, but what happens if you use a gear half the size? Put marks on the gears to determine RPMs or gear ratios. Circumferences might also need to be determined.

(c) 2017 MediaStream Press

50 STEAM Labs

Laser Light Show — 21

SCIENCE: Research light, visible and invisible light spectrums, and lasers. Also look into refraction and reflection, as well as opaque, translucent, and transparent objects and how they can affect light.

TECHNOLOGY: Use laser pointers or other light sources. Record video or take pictures of the lighting effects you create.

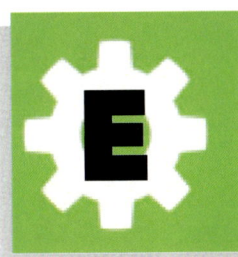

ENGINEERING: Arrange mirrors and other reflective objects. Shine a variety of laser pointers or light sources off of them to create interesting effects. Also try containers of different liquids in differently-shaped containers to see how they affect light.

ART: Create an album of pictures, slideshow, light show, or other visual arts project to go with your research and experimentation.

MATHEMATICS: Calculate angles of refraction or determine how many times complicated prisms or crystals split light. Use geometry and patterns to predict what will happen when additional mirrors or prisms are added. Attempt to make geometric shapes with laser light, prisms or mirrors, and dark rooms.

(c) 2017 MediaStream Press

50 STEAM Labs

Heavy Hitters — 22

SCIENCE: Research force and motion, as well as Newton's Laws. How are they involved in a specific sport or in a variety of sports?

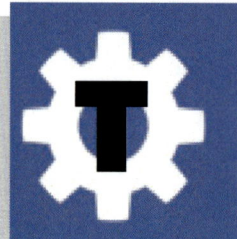

TECHNOLOGY: Watch videos of trick plays, amazing shots, and other sports highlights videos. How would these change if the game mechanics change?

ENGINEERING: Design or experiment with a variety of sizes and styles of sports equipment. Switch up the sizes of balls when trying volleyball, change a puck for a ball in hockey, golf with a larger ball, or try bowling with pins in a different arrangement.

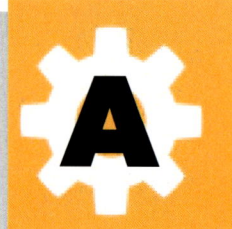

ART: Sketch and design alternative ideas for a sport. What other ways could equipment such as helmets, pads, sticks, bats, or balls look?

MATHEMATICS: Find stats about the sizes and weights of balls, pucks, bats, and sticks in various sports. Make comparative charts and tables.

(c) 2017 MediaStream Press

50 STEAM Labs

 **STEAM Bloggers**  23

 **SCIENCE:** Research a science topic you are interested in. Prepare a brief article or reflection about it, to be shared online.

 **TECHNOLOGY:** Create a blog or series of blog entries on a class or approved blog. Include at least 2 elements of STEAM in every post.

 **ENGINEERING:** Try to have a video or photos of a physical project in one or more posts. Show the steps of building, or the actual results of a test.

 **ART:** Design the look of the post. Add graphics and visual media to it to increase visual interest.

 **MATHEMATICS:** Add measurement and data to one or more posts. Track responses and the number of views.

(c) 2017 MediaStream Press

50 STEAM Labs

 # Time Jumpers  24

 **SCIENCE:** Research the history and science behind your item.

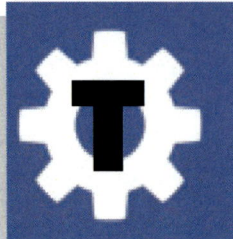 **TECHNOLOGY:** Make a slideshow, presentation, or video blog about the creation process.

 **ENGINEERING:** Redesign a common item to look old-fashioned or futuristic. Build a prototype or model.

 **ART:** Sketch blueprints, design, and decorate a prototype.

 **MATHEMATICS:** Create your model to actual scale, blow it up for better visual inspection, or shrink it down to make it manageable. Prove with measurements that your model is to scale. What is the ratio of size to the original?

(c) 2017 MediaStream Press

50 STEAM Labs

Fine Furnishings 25

SCIENCE: Research the science and materials involved in creating a piece of furniture. Plan a variation of it, updated in your own style or make a futuristic version of it.

TECHNOLOGY: Create a media comparison that shows why yours is the better version. Like a pitch or piece of persuasive media, convince people that your product is better.

ENGINEERING: Create a full-size or model of your proposed piece of furniture. Explain the differences between materials used in both styles. For example: if you're switching from chromed steel to aluminum, explain the differences, or explain the differences in two types of wood being used.

ART: Sketch blueprints, design, and decorate a prototype. Make it visually appealing. Optionally, create a furniture brochure advertisement.

MATHEMATICS: Create detailed sketches showing the measurements of the original and of your new version (either proposed or actual built model). Create a comparative chart to show the differences and similarities in measurements. Make a write-up explaining cost.

(c) 2017 MediaStream Press

50 STEAM Labs

Aerodynamics 26

SCIENCE: Research aerodynamics, especially as it relates to plane or car design.

TECHNOLOGY: Use high speed or slow motion photography to capture evidence of wind patterns around objects in the tunnel.

ENGINEERING: Create a wind tunnel using available materials. Test objects in the tunnel. What can you add to make the wind patterns visible with slow motion photography?

ART: Slow motion photography will be needed to capture the wind patterns in the tunnel. What can be released to watch the wind swirl around model cars or airplanes?

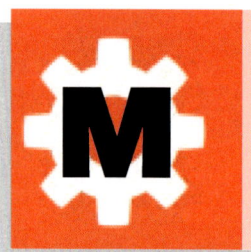

MATHEMATICS: Calculate wind speed in your tunnel at different settings.

(c) 2017 MediaStream Press

50 STEAM Labs

Derby Races   27

SCIENCE: Research speed and velocity. Also research the speeds of typical cars, race cars, and the fastest land speed records.

TECHNOLOGY: Use stopwatches to record race times. Photography can be used to provide photo finishes.

ENGINEERING: Build a track with at least 2 lanes. The track should be long enough to test cars running down it. Test the track with model cars or toy cars.

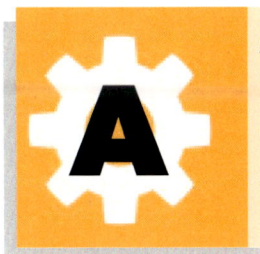

ART: Slow motion photography will be needed to capture the wind patterns in the tunnel. What can be released to watch the wind swirl around model cars or airplanes?

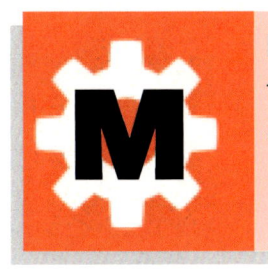

MATHEMATICS: Record race times and use them to calculate velocities of the cars. Graph and chart data. Additionally, speeds of land animals, people, and land vehicles can be charted to show comparisons.

(c) 2017 MediaStream Press

50 STEAM Labs

 Future Tech  28

 **SCIENCE:** Research a famous inventor, as well as inventions similar to the one you want to create.

 **TECHNOLOGY:** Use libraries, the internet, and other resources to research inventions and get ideas for your own. Also learn about patents.

 **ENGINEERING:** Create a model of your invention, working if possible.

 **ART:** Sketch, design, and create blueprints for your invention.

 **MATHEMATICS:** Give measurement statistics for your invention, as well as any other applicable mathematical data.

(c) 2017 MediaStream Press

50 STEAM Labs

Let's Make Music

  29

SCIENCE: Research acoustics and the movement of sound. Also look into how different types of instruments generate sound. How are families of instruments similar?

TECHNOLOGY: Record a sample of your instrument's music to share.

ENGINEERING: Design a playable original instrument capable of creating as many tones as possible.

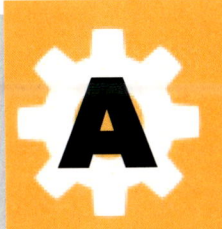
ART: Compose an original piece of music, or play a classic tune on your new instrument, comparing it to the same song played on a more traditional instrument.

MATHEMATICS: Calculate the measurement statistics of your instrument. Also, if it can create multiple tones, are there any measurements that help create these, such as longer/shorter strings or narrower/wider tubes? Also, create a timeline of instruments, showing the older ones all the way to more modern instruments.

(c) 2017 MediaStream Press

50 STEAM Labs

Block Marvels

  30

 **SCIENCE:** Research the processes involved in creating building toys. What materials are used? What machines are required?

 **TECHNOLOGY:** Make a slideshow, blog post, or presentation about building toys.

 **ENGINEERING:** Create a machine using building block toys. It should be capable of movement and may include gears, spring drives, or something of that sort.

 **ART:** Decorate your machine to suit its purpose.

 **MATHEMATICS:** Calculate meaningful statistics of your device, such as gear ratios, movement distances, or the time it takes to complete one cycle of its movement. A timeline or graph of the invention of building toys can also be created.

(c) 2017 MediaStream Press

50 STEAM Labs

Media Mammals

31

SCIENCE: Research mammals. Choose one to do a project on.

TECHNOLOGY: Make a multimedia presentation of your mammal, including video clips and sounds when possible. This will go along with a model of an animal, as well as any props that can be shared, like feathers, scales, claws, or furs.

ENGINEERING: Create a scale or real-sized model of your mammal, or a part of it, such as a flipper, face, claw, etc... Adding movement or working parts is a plus!

ART: Create and decorate your model for accuracy and realism.

MATHEMATICS: Research mathematical facts about your mammal, such as weight, length/height, lifespan, conservation status...

(c) 2017 MediaStream Press

50 STEAM Labs

Monument Makers 32

SCIENCE: Research the building processes involved in the monument.

TECHNOLOGY: Research a famous world monument. Prepare a slideshow, blog post, presentation, or multimedia piece to accompany a project.

ENGINEERING: Build a scale model or diorama of a monument.

ART: Create the best model of a monument as you can from available materials. Decorate for realism. Adding little people, landscaping, and nature around it is a plus!

MATHEMATICS: Calculate the scale of your project. What size ratio is it? How does the model's weight and measurements compare to the real thing? A timeline explaining the milestones of the monument's creation can also be created.

(c) 2017 MediaStream Press

50 STEAM Labs

Green Living

  33

SCIENCE: Research greenhouses and hot house growing techniques. Determine watering, drainage, and other basic needs for your plants and how to best supply them.

TECHNOLOGY: Make a blueprint of your greenhouse with a piece of illustration or 3D modeling software. You can also draw it first and then add notes and measurements to a scanned photo with software.

ENGINEERING: Build a greenhouse or a model of a greenhouse. Test it!

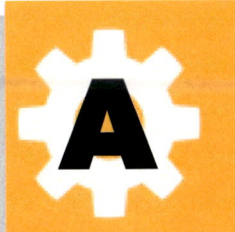
ART: Use recycled materials or other cast-offs to make and/or decorate the greenhouse. Artistically arrange herbs, flowers, and other plants inside it.

MATHEMATICS: Measure the volume of soil, area of growing space, and other statistics of your greenhouse.

(c) 2017 MediaStream Press

50 STEAM Labs

Bridge Masters   34

 **SCIENCE:** Research different types of bridges, like truss, suspension, beam, arch, etc... Learn how weight is distributes to allow the bridge to stay together and hold as weight crosses it.

 **TECHNOLOGY:** Make a presentation, blog post, or other project showing major types of bridges and record-breaking bridges of different eras.

 **ENGINEERING:** Design and build a model bridge from available materials.

 **ART:** Sketch and draw plans for your bridge. Paint and decorate it for realism.

 **MATHEMATICS:** Test your bridge against criteria, such as the amount of weight that can be held, the longest distance it can span while remaining within certain measurement constraints, etc...

(c) 2017 MediaStream Press

50 STEAM Labs

View Masters — 35

SCIENCE: Research kaleidoscopes, telescopes, microscopes, binoculars, eyeglasses, or other optical devices. How do they work? How do they use lenses or mirrors to accomplish their goals?

TECHNOLOGY: Create a project or presentation relating to optics.

ENGINEERING: Create an optical device or tool that can be used to magnify or see at a distance.

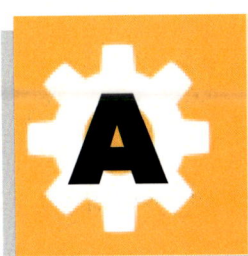

ART: Create a piece of photographic art dealing with zoom, magnification, or focus.

MATHEMATICS: Create a timeline of inventions and discoveries relating to optics. Also, magnification comparisons can be created, such as a 10x zoom of a basic object as compared to its normal viewing state.

(c) 2017 MediaStream Press

# Space Race   36

SCIENCE: Research rocketry and the forces of flight. Also look into the G-forces humans might encounter during different situations, such as riding a rollercoaster, flying a jet plane, riding a rocket into space, etc...

TECHNOLOGY: Put together a multimedia report on rocketry over the ages, especially as mankind began reaching for space.

ENGINEERING: Design and build a rocket that can shoot as high as possible using safe propulsion methods, like air, water, or rubber bands. Safety measures should be observed.

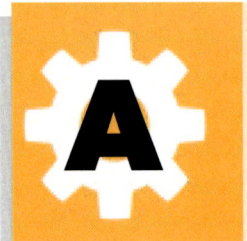

ART: Create an infographic showing the takeoffs, travels, and landings of your rockets. Also, decorate your finished rocket. You can even make up your own space agency logo.

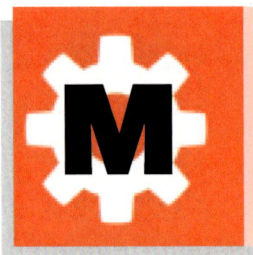

MATHEMATICS: Calculate the heights and distances traveled during multiple tests of your rocket(s). Graph them or create tables or infographics. Also, the G-forces of different methods of flight can be assembled in a table, or the speeds different planes and rockets travel at can be charted and graphed.

50 STEAM Labs

Walking Wounded — 37

SCIENCE: Research prosthetics, braces, and other rehabilitative measures people used when recovering from injuries. Research different types of joints and the bones/muscles of the human body. Also note that prosthetic limbs have been developed for animals.

TECHNOLOGY: Create a music video, video montage, or other multimedia project showcasing different types of prosthetic limbs. 3D renderings of your designs are also a possibility.

ENGINEERING: Make a model or prototype of a prosthetic limb.

ART: Create a collage of prosthetic limbs used in humans and animals. Design some of your own.

MATHEMATICS: Find statistics about prosthetic limbs. Also, you can find statistics and measurements about your own designs.

(c) 2017 MediaStream Press

50 STEAM Labs

Golden Records — 38

SCIENCE: Research a science topic of your choice to create a science song.

TECHNOLOGY: Record a science song! Either make an original tune and record it, or use a karaoke version of a song without words, and record your own lyrics to make a science parody of another song.

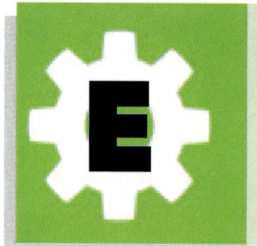

ENGINEERING: Create a microphone box lined with foam or other materials. Record from a variety of locations, in different boxes, and with different materials lining the boxes to learn about different acoustics.

ART: Design a case or container to showcase your burned mp3, or decorate a flash drive.

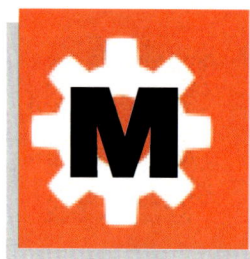

MATHEMATICS: If possible, write sheet music or lyrical notes to show the beats, measures, and times of your song.

(c) 2017 MediaStream Press

50 STEAM Labs

Bikers — 39

SCIENCE: Research gears, chain drives, and simple machines involved in bicycles.

TECHNOLOGY: Create a multimedia advertisement to sell your super cool bike.

ENGINEERING: Create a model of a bicycle. If possible, make some of the gears work, the handlebars turn, and include some sort of braking mechanism.

ART: Make the bike look extra cool. It needs a serious paint job. Also, carefully craft your advertisement to make the bike look great.

MATHEMATICS: Calculate the cost of building your model. Determine its scale and general measurements. Make a rough calculation of the cost to make a larger one in real size if the cost was proportionate.

(c) 2017 MediaStream Press

Balloons 40

SCIENCE: Research hot air balloons and high altitude weather balloons.

TECHNOLOGY: If possible, use a small camera (that you could potentially afford to lose) or drone to record the flight of your balloon. Also, try locating on online map services and then printing out a satellite image of your school yard, home, or local park where you launch from. Then

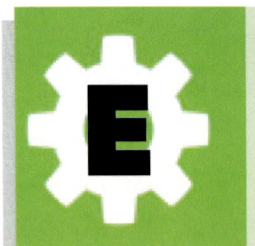

ENGINEERING: Design a hot air balloon. Build it. Safely use candle light or solar heat to make it fly.

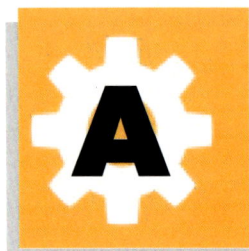

ART: Make your balloon look super awesome. Also, blueprints and plans can be drawn up.

MATHEMATICS: Make a timeline of balloon-related inventions and milestones. Also, graph, chart, or otherwise record flight data from your balloon.

Alternative Energy 41

SCIENCE: Research alternative energy sources, such as wind and solar power. Also look into how machines are powered and how energy is transferred through liquids and air (hydraulic and pneumatic power).

TECHNOLOGY: Take photos to make an album or photographic timeline of experimentation and assembly.

ENGINEERING: Design a device that is powered by water, air, or other non-electrical sources. It can't simply be hand-cranked or man-powered, either. Pneumatic, hydraulic, or solar powered devices are acceptable.

ART: Add color to the project. For example, the hydraulic fluid can be colorful, possibly even mixing somewhere in the project. Different colored disks moving and crossing to show different colors is also an option.

MATHEMATICS: Find something measurable in your project, such as: RPMs for a moving part of your project, PSI in within your hydraulic project, or other applicable facts.

50 STEAM Labs

So Very Hungry — 42

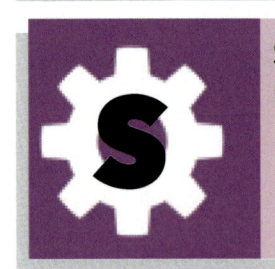

SCIENCE: Research agricultural techniques, how a specific ingredient is harvested, or how a type of food is created.

TECHNOLOGY: Make a presentation about a specific food you like.

ENGINEERING: Design a project dealing with food! It can make food, cook food, separate food, or be built from food.

ART: Found art project - use food and food wrappers to make a piece of art to accompany your project.

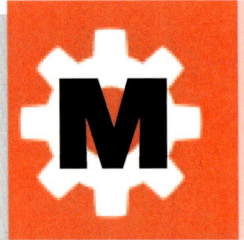

MATHEMATICS: Calculate nutritional information for a specific food or for several foods. Compare it to other foods. Create proportions and graphs to show its healthfulness or unhealthiness. What nutrients is the food high in?

(c) 2017 MediaStream Press

50 STEAM Labs

Outdoor Games   43

SCIENCE: Research forces, motion, or science concepts applicable to your game.

TECHNOLOGY: Make a fun rules brochure or video demonstration for your game.

ENGINEERING: Design and build an outdoor game. Either make a larger, outdoor version of an existing game, or create a new team game or party game. Create it from available or affordable materials.

ART: Make your game colorful and entertaining.

MATHEMATICS: Create a scoring system for your game. Keep track. Scoring record sheets can also be made to help keep score as you play.

(c) 2017 MediaStream Press

50 STEAM Labs

Get Baking — 44

SCIENCE: Research chemical reactions, as well as compounds and elements. One particular reaction to look into is baking soda + vinegar.

TECHNOLOGY: Record a video of your project using baking soda and vinegar to cause movement or changes.

ENGINEERING: Design a project that is powered by the release of gases during the reaction of baking soda and vinegar. As the gas is released, it should cause some sort of movement or change in your project.

ART: Add color and fun to your project and your presentation. Make fun signs and other decorations for background and accents/storyboards during your video.

MATHEMATICS: Calculate the reaction's difference with differing amounts of vinegar and baking soda. Which proportion is most successful. Chart or graph your results.

(c) 2017 MediaStream Press

50 STEAM Labs

Cardbored... 45

SCIENCE: Research recycling, how cardboard is made, and how cardboard is reused.

TECHNOLOGY: Create a presentation showcasing your project.

ENGINEERING: Design a project made primarily from reused cardboard boxes of varying sizes and shapes.

ART: Paint and decorate your project.

MATHEMATICS: Find the dimensions of each of your boxes. Use the measurements to calculate the volumes and surface areas of each.

(c) 2017 MediaStream Press

50 STEAM Labs

Rainbow Makers — 46

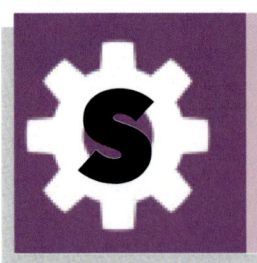

SCIENCE: Research light, the visible spectrum, and refraction.

TECHNOLOGY: Make a multimedia presentation about light.

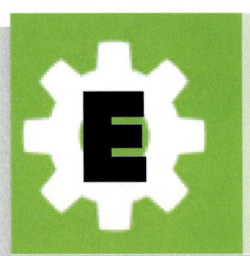

ENGINEERING: Fill several containers of similar or different shapes and sizes with a variety of colors, all the shades of rainbows. See what happens when shining light and laser pointers through them.

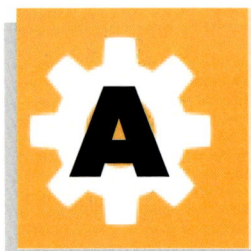

ART: Make a series of illustrations showing what occurs when you shine the lights through the colored water.

MATHEMATICS: Measure angles of refraction, count how many times the light is split by the shapes of the containers, and find other math facts about your project.

(c) 2017 MediaStream Press

Photographers 47

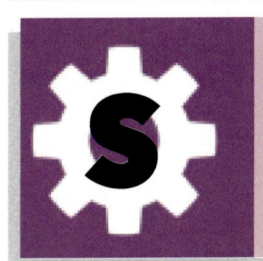

SCIENCE: Research how photography works, especially the kind with film. What chemical reactions are involved in processing film, including polaroid film.

TECHNOLOGY: Use a camera in different lighting settings to see how colors of light, amounts of light, reflections, and other effects of lighting effect pictures. Create a showcase of your best effects.

ENGINEERING: Set up lighting with different colors, angles, and intensities. Also try different types of light bulbs, multiple light sources, and natural vs. indoor lighting.

ART: Stage and set up photo shoots. Use props, people, and nature to make the best photos possible.

MATHEMATICS: Use a photometer if possible to measure the lighting conditions. Or, create a ratio or set of statistics to explain how many pictures turned out from each set and each lighting situation.

50 STEAM Labs

Famous Painters 48

SCIENCE: Research the ingredients in paints. How are paints made? What are the different types of paints? Also look into solubility, solutions, mixtures, and suspensions.

TECHNOLOGY: Create a multimedia showcase of your artwork.

ENGINEERING: Design a series of painting tools or devices as alternatives to paint brushes. Test and use them.

ART: Create artwork with your custom painting tools. Use mixed media if possible. You can also paint as a response to a piece of reading or music.

MATHEMATICS: Use graduated containers to measure how much paint your devices pick up each time. Which ones use the most? the least?

(c) 2017 MediaStream Press

50 STEAM Labs

Sticking Around — 49

SCIENCE: Research cement and adhesives, as well as chemical reactions.

TECHNOLOGY: Record or film clips of your tests and attempts. Commentate and explain what is occurring.

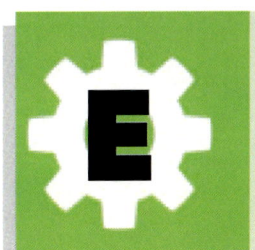

ENGINEERING: Design a series of tests for different surfaces and different adhesives. Test to see how well things stick together. How do the two objects survive being pried apart or peeled away from each other?

ART: Create a presentation board featuring some of your objects that were glued together and peeled apart.

MATHEMATICS: Come up with a scale or set of measures to determine success rates of adhesives on surfaces. Chart and graph data.

(c) 2017 MediaStream Press

50 STEAM Labs

Music for the Mind — 50

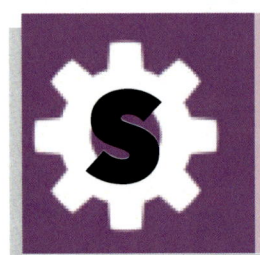

SCIENCE: Research acoustics, musical theory, and other music and sound related topics.

TECHNOLOGY: Record any music or noises you've created. Create a presentation about your findings.

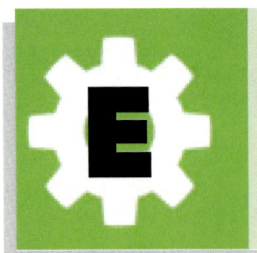

ENGINEERING: Create a project related to music. It could be behavioral science, studying the effects of music on people or animals. It might also be a project on creating noises and music from objects.

ART: Create music or noises. You can also trying matching them to words, colors, pictures, or other stimuli.

MATHEMATICS: Record statistics about your music, such as the duration, beats per minute, timing, etc... Chart or graph the results of your project, if possible.

(c) 2017 MediaStream Press

Blank Templates

Make your own STEAM Labs on the following pages! Five copies have been included. However, you are granted a limited license to reproduce as many of these blank forms as you need for home or classroom use.

Please support this project by sharing with colleagues only limited samples from within. For more information about licensing or other requests, please email: mediastreampressllc@gmail.com

50 STEAM Labs

SCIENCE:

TECHNOLOGY:

ENGINEERING:

ART:

MATHEMATICS:

(c) 2017 MediaStream Press

50 STEAM Labs

SCIENCE:

TECHNOLOGY:

ENGINEERING:

ART:

MATHEMATICS:

(c) 2017 MediaStream Press

50 STEAM Labs

SCIENCE:

TECHNOLOGY:

ENGINEERING:

ART:

MATHEMATICS:

(c) 2017 MediaStream Press

50 STEAM Labs

SCIENCE:

TECHNOLOGY:

ENGINEERING:

ART:

MATHEMATICS:

(c) 2017 MediaStream Press

50 STEAM Labs

SCIENCE:

TECHNOLOGY:

ENGINEERING:

ART:

MATHEMATICS:

(c) 2017 MediaStream Press

Andrew Frinkle

Andrew Frinkle is an award-nominated teacher and writer with experience in America and overseas, as well as years developing educational materials for big name educational sites like Have Fun Teaching. He has taught PreK all the way up to adult classes, and has focused on ESOL/EFL techniques, as well as STEM Education. With two young children at home now, he's been developing more and more teaching strategies and books aimed at helping young learners.

Andrew Frinkle is the founder & owner of MediaStream Press LLC www.MediaStreamPress.com, a game, book, and media publishing company. MediaStream Press maintains the following educational websites:
www.50STEMLabs.com
www.common-core-assessments.com
www.littlelearninglabs.com

He also writes fantasy and science fiction novels under the pen name Velerion Damarke and writes/illustrates children's fiction as Andrew Frinkle. Find out more at:
www.underspace.org
www.AndrewFrinkle.com

MediaStream Press

PUBLISHING: MediaStream Press has over educational 100 titles available on Amazon, as well as over 20 novels and children's books. Search for the authors: Andrew Frinkle (educational and illustrated children's books) or Velerion Damarke (fiction).

www.MediaStreamPress.com
www.50STEMLabs.com
www.AndrewFrinkle.com
www.common-core-assessments.com
www.LittleLearningLabs.com
www.underspace.org

Made in the USA
Lexington, KY
10 July 2018